BETTER WITH
BEER

ISBN-13: 978-1-56383-578-0
Item #7154

Printed in the USA
<u>Distributed By:</u>

507 Industrial Street
Waverly, IA 50677

www.cqbookstore.com

gifts@cqbookstore.com

 CQ Products

 CQ Products

 @cqproducts

 @cqproducts

It's time to take that frothy goodness into the kitchen!

Cooking with beer just makes sense – it's packed with built-in flavor, you probably already have a few on hand, and it's one versatile beverage in the kitchen! Your favorite brewskie can be used for baking, deglazing, marinating, simmering, saucing, and *(of course)* sipping. Whether it's breakfast, lunch, dinner, or dessert, cooking with beer easily transforms a meal by adding complexity and depth to the flavor. Who knew beer was the secret to great-tasting food?

So go on, pop a top and let beer infiltrate every part of the meal... you know you want to! After all, everything is *Better with Beer*!

Lager Marinated Steak Tacos

1 (12 oz.) bottle
  LIGHT LAGER
Juice of 2 limes
2 T. olive oil
1 tsp. red pepper flakes
½ tsp. garlic salt
½ tsp. salt
½ tsp. black pepper

2 lbs. beef flat iron steak
1 red onion, sliced
12 corn tortillas
2 avocados, sliced
¼ C. chopped cilantro
¼ C. cotija cheese,
  crumbled
Lime wedges

In a large resealable bag, mix the light lager, lime juice, olive oil, red pepper flakes, garlic salt, salt, and black pepper until combined. Add the steak and onions to the marinade and turn to coat. Refrigerate for at least 30 minutes.

Move the oven rack 6" from the heating element and preheat the broiler. Preheat a cast iron grill pan by placing it in the oven for 15 to 20 minutes.

Pull out the oven rack and lay the steak and onions on the pan and discard the marinade. Broil about 4 minutes on each side, or until the steak reaches the desired doneness and the onions are crisp-tender.

Let the steak rest for 5 minutes before cutting diagonally across the grain into thin slices. Serve on corn tortillas with the grilled onions, avocados, cilantro, and cotija cheese. Use the lime wedges for drizzling.

Tavern Cookies

1 (12 oz.) bottle **STOUT**

¾ C. unsalted butter, cubed

⅔ C. packed brown sugar

½ C. sugar

1 egg, plus 1 yolk

1 tsp. vanilla extract

1 C. all-purpose flour

¾ C. bread flour

1 tsp. cornstarch

½ tsp. baking soda

¼ tsp. salt

1 C. dark chocolate chips

½ C. broken pretzels

¼ C. dry-roasted peanuts

Add the stout to a pot over medium heat and simmer, stirring occasionally, until reduced to about 2 tablespoons of liquid, about 15 to 20 minutes.

In the bowl of a stand mixer, add the butter and both types of sugar; beat together until creamed. Add the egg and the yolk and mix until well combined. Add the stout reduction and vanilla extract and beat until combined, scraping the bottom to make sure all the ingredients are mixed.

In a separate bowl, whisk together both types of flour, cornstarch, baking soda, and salt. Add the dry ingredients to the stand mixer bowl and mix on medium speed until just barely combined. Add the chocolate chips, pretzels, and peanuts and stir to incorporate.

Cover a rimmed baking sheet with parchment paper; scoop the dough and roll into golf ball-sized rounds. Place on the baking sheet, cover with plastic wrap, and chill for at least 3 hours.

Preheat the oven to 350°.

Bake for 16 to 21 minutes or until golden brown.

Short & Stout

*Pour 6 oz. **stout**, 1 oz. Irish cream, and 1 oz. chocolate syrup into a lowball glass and stir to combine. Add enough ice to fill the glass. Yum! Who knew so much flavor could be packed into such a little glass? Serves 1*

Serves 6

Beer Brat Potatchos

1 lb. bratwurst

2 (12 oz.) cans
   AMERICAN LAGER

1 C. cream cheese

2 C. shredded cheddar
   cheese

¼ tsp. garlic salt

¼ tsp. cayenne pepper

2 T. Dijon mustard

½ T. black pepper

¼ tsp. salt

1 (8 oz.) bag kettle-cooked
   potato chips

1 C. sauerkraut,
   drained & squeezed

½ C. Flamin' Beer
   Jalapeños
   (recipe on page 9)

Chopped chives

In a large skillet, brown the bratwurst on both sides over medium-high heat. Add both cans of American lager to the skillet; simmer over medium-low heat for 20 minutes. Remove the bratwurst from the skillet, slice, and set aside.

Continue to simmer the beer over medium-low; add the cream cheese and cheddar cheese to the skillet. Stir occasionally until mixture is smooth. Add the garlic salt, cayenne pepper, mustard, black pepper, and salt; stir to incorporate.

Spread the chips on a serving platter and top with the beer cheese, bratwurst slices, sauerkraut, and jalapeños; garnish with chives.

Flamin' Beer Jalapeños

Add 5 to 6 thinly sliced jalapeños and 2 cloves of garlic to a glass jar.

In a saucepan over medium heat, combine 1 C. **IPA**, 1 C. apple cider vinegar, 3 T. sugar, 2 tsp. salt, and 1 T. black peppercorns; stir until the salt and sugar dissolve. Remove from heat and pour the pickling liquid over the jalapeños. Cover and refrigerate for 24 hours. The jalapeños will last for several weeks in the refrigerator.

Irish Stout Treats

3 T. butter

5 C. miniature
   marshmallows

⅓ C. Irish cream

6 C. crisped rice cereal

½ C. **STOUT**

1 T. whiskey

¼ C. dark chocolate chips

2 C. powdered sugar

1 tsp. unsweetened
   cocoa powder

Spray a 9 x 13" pan with cooking spray.

Melt the butter in saucepan over low heat. Add the marshmallows and stir until melted. Remove from the heat; add the Irish cream and stir until mixed. Add the crisped rice cereal and stir until completely coated.

Press the cereal mixture into the greased pan and place in the refrigerator to cool for at least 20 minutes.

Meanwhile, heat the stout and whiskey in a small saucepan over medium heat until reduced by about half. Add the chocolate chips and stir until melted. Put the powdered sugar and cocoa powder into a small bowl and add the stout reduction, one tablespoon at a time, and whisk until it reaches the consistency of a thick glaze that can be drizzled onto the treats *(you may not use all of the stout reduction)*. Drizzle the treats with the stout glaze and cut into squares.

Shirley's Secret

*In a highball glass filled with ice, combine 1 oz. grenadine, 2 oz. lemonade, and 6 oz. **light lager**. Gently stir to combine; garnish with a maraschino cherry and a slice of lemon. You'll love this grown-up twist on a Shirley Temple! Serves 1*

Serves 6

Beer-Braised Brussels

Wash and trim the ends off of 2 lbs. Brussels sprouts; cut the sprouts in half and set aside. Add 8 slices chopped bacon to a large skillet over medium heat and sauté until crisp; drain the drippings and set the bacon aside to cool.

Add 1 thinly sliced shallot to the skillet and sauté for 2 to 3 minutes to soften, then add the Brussels sprouts. Sauté for 4 to 5 minutes. Pour 1 bottle of **AMBER ALE** into the skillet. Add ½ tsp. salt, ¼ tsp. black pepper, 1 T. honey, and ¼ tsp. crushed red pepper. Bring to a simmer and lower the heat. Stir and simmer until the beer has reduced to a glaze and the sprouts are cooked through, about 15 minutes.

Brewpub Mac

Add 8 slices chopped bacon to a large skillet over medium heat; sauté until crisp and set aside to drain. Cook 1 (16 oz.) box of macaroni according to package directions for al dente; drain and set aside. In a large pot, melt ¼ C. butter over medium-high heat. Add 1 tsp. minced garlic, ¼ C. all-purpose flour, 1 tsp. salt, ½ tsp. black pepper, and ½ tsp. paprika; stirring until smooth. Whisk in 2½ C. milk, 1 C. AMBER ALE, and ¼ C. heavy cream. Bring to a boil and stir until thickened.

Reduce heat. Add 2 C. each shredded Gouda and shredded cheddar cheese and stir until melted. Add the macaroni and half of the crumbled bacon and stir to combine. Top with the remaining bacon and chives.

Serves 5

Belgian Ale Waffles

2 C. flour

1 tsp. baking powder

½ tsp. baking soda

¼ tsp. salt

2 T. sugar

2 large eggs, lightly beaten

1 C. **BELGIAN-STYLE WHITE ALE**

¾ C. milk

¼ C. butter, melted

½ tsp. vanilla extract

1 tsp. orange zest, plus more for garnish

Powdered sugar

Whipped cream

Maple syrup

Preheat waffle iron according to manufacturer directions.

In a large bowl, whisk together the flour, baking powder, baking soda, salt, and sugar; set aside.

In a separate bowl, combine the eggs, Belgian-style white ale, milk, butter, vanilla extract, and orange zest. Add the egg mixture to the flour mixture and fold together until just combined. Cook the waffles according to manufacturer directions.

Serve warm, topped with powdered sugar, whipped cream, maple syrup, and orange zest.

Beer in waffles... who would've guessed? Belgian-style white ales are flavored with orange peel, coriander, and other subtle spice notes. This makes them a great addition to citrusy recipes and desserts.

Brunch Punch

*Add 4 oz. orange juice, 6 oz. **light lager**, and 1 oz. amaretto to a pint glass. Stir together and add enough ice to fill the glass. Garnish with an orange slice. No need to feel guilty, the orange juice makes this cocktail part of a well-balanced breakfast. Serves 1*

Makes 40-50

Beer-Boiled Shrimp

2 qts. water

2 C. **IPA**

Juice of 1 lemon

1 T. salt

1 lb. medium shrimp

1 T. seafood seasoning

IPA Curry Mayo *(recipe on page 17)*

In a large pot, bring the water, IPA, lemon juice, and salt to a boil; turn down the heat to a simmer. If needed, devein and peel the shrimp, leaving the tails intact for easy dipping. Add the shrimp and the seafood seasoning to the pot. Cook for a few minutes until the shrimp are opaque, pink and cooked through.

Drain and rinse the shrimp under cold running water to cool. Store covered in the refrigerator until ready to serve. Serve chilled with IPA Curry Mayo.

Who doesn't love an easy recipe with a high "wow" factor? Just whip these bad boys up ahead of time and let them chill until the party starts. Guests will be impressed, and you'll be able to step back, grab a beer, and enjoy the party.

IPA Curry Mayo

Combine 1 C. mayonnaise, 1 T. curry powder, 2 T. **IPA**, juice of ½ lime, ¼ C. chopped cilantro, and 1 tsp. salt; mix well. Serve with Beer-Boiled Shrimp.

Makes 24

White Ale Citrus Cupcakes

2½ C. all-purpose flour

2 tsp. baking powder

½ tsp. salt

¾ C. plus 6 T. unsalted butter, softened, divided

1¾ C. sugar

3 eggs

1 tsp. vanilla extract

1½ tsp. orange zest, divided

¼ C. milk

1 (12 oz.) bottle **BELGIAN-STYLE WHITE ALE**, divided

12 oz. cream cheese, softened

1 T. orange juice

4 C. powdered sugar

Orange wedges

Preheat the oven to 375° and line 24 standard muffin cups with liners.

In a small bowl, combine the milk and 1 cup Belgian-style white ale.

In a large mixing bowl, whisk together flour, baking powder, and salt and set aside. With an electric mixer, beat together ¾ cup butter and the sugar for 2 to 3 minutes or until fluffy. Add the eggs one at a time, beating well after each addition. Mix in the vanilla extract and ½ teaspoon orange zest. Alternately add the dry and wet ingredients to the butter mixture with the mixer on low, beginning and ending with the dry ingredients.

Fill each cupcake liner ⅔ full and bake for 18 minutes, or until a toothpick comes out clean. While they are still warm, poke holes in the top of each cupcake with a toothpick and brush the remainder of the beer on top.

For the frosting, mix the cream cheese and the remaining 6 tablespoons butter with an electric mixer. Beat in the orange juice and 1 teaspoon orange zest. Gradually add the powdered sugar, beating until smooth.

Using a piping bag fitted with a star tip, pipe the frosting onto cooled cupcakes. Garnish with orange wedges and zest.

Irish Iced Latte

*Mix 2 oz. cold coffee, 6 oz. **stout**, ½ oz. whiskey, and 1 oz. simple syrup* in a highball glass. Add enough ice to fill the glass. Gently drizzle 1 oz. heavy cream into the glass so it slowly sinks into coffee. Serves 1.*

* Make simple syrup by combining equal amounts sugar and water in a small saucepan over medium heat until the sugar dissolves. Cool before using.

Serves 10

Watermelon Brewskie Punch

Remove and discard the rind of a large seedless watermelon and roughly chop the fruit into 2" pieces. Place the watermelon in a food processor and pulse until liquefied. Pour through a mesh strainer to remove the pulp. Discard the pulp and repeat the process until the whole watermelon has been blended. You should end up with roughly 6 C. of watermelon juice. Add 2 T. sugar and 1 (12 oz.) can frozen limeade to the juice and stir until dissolved. Refrigerate until ready to use.

When ready to serve, transfer the juice to a large pitcher. Add 4 (12 oz.) bottles of **LIGHT LAGER** and 8 oz. cherry vodka and stir to combine. Serve over ice.

Hot & Hopped Hummus

Add 2 stemmed and seeded jalapeños, 3 T. tahini paste, 1½ C. canned garbanzo beans *(drained and rinsed)*, ⅓ C. chopped cilantro, 1 T. olive oil, juice of 1 lime, ½ tsp. minced garlic, ½ tsp. onion powder, ½ tsp. salt, ½ tsp. cayenne pepper, and ⅓ C. **IPA** to a food processor. Process until smooth and well mixed. Serve with pita or tortilla chips for dipping.

Makes 12 Cups

Pubbed Caramel Corn

2 (3.5 oz.) bags
microwavable popcorn,
popped

1 C. chopped pecans

1 C. crushed pretzels

1 (12 oz.) bottle
BROWN ALE

3 T. unsalted butter

2 C. brown sugar

1 C. heavy cream

¼ tsp. salt

2 tsp. vanilla extract

½ tsp. baking soda

Preheat oven to 250°.

Spread the popped popcorn, pecans, and pretzels on a large, foil-lined rimmed baking sheet; place in the oven to keep warm.

Add the brown ale and butter to a saucepan and bring to a low boil. Add the brown sugar and boil until it looks like thick syrup; stir in the cream until combined. Continue to cook for about 5 minutes or until caramel thickens.

Remove from the heat and add the salt, vanilla extract, and baking soda. Remove the popcorn mixture from the oven and add the caramel; mix until everything is well coated.

Return to the oven and bake for 1 hour, stirring every 15 minutes.

Spread the caramel corn mixture on parchment paper to cool. Store in an airtight container.

Moscow Shandy

*Combine 6 oz. **American lager**, 4 oz. ginger beer, 1 oz. vodka, and the juice of ½ lime in a cocktail glass. Add ¼ tsp. of freshly grated ginger to the glass and stir to combine. Add ice to fill and garnish with a slice of lime. Delish! Serves 1*

Hopped-Up Lemon Bars

1¼ C. flour, divided

⅓ C. powdered sugar, plus more for dusting

6 T. unsalted butter

¼ tsp. salt

3 eggs

1½ C. sugar

2 T. cornstarch

¼ C. freshly squeezed lemon juice

⅓ C. **IPA**

1 tsp. lemon zest

Preheat oven to 350°.

Add 1 cup flour, powdered sugar, butter, and salt to a food processor. Process until well combined. Press into the bottom of a greased 8 x 8" pan. Chill for 15 minutes.

Bake the crust for 20 to 25 minutes or until golden brown. Remove from the oven and cool to room temperature.

In a large bowl, whisk together the eggs, sugar, the remaining ¼ cup flour, and cornstarch. Add the lemon juice, IPA, and zest; stir until combined. Pour the filling over the cooled crust. Bake at 350° until the center has set, about 25 to 30 minutes. Allow to cool slightly before refrigerating. Chill for 2 to 3 hours before cutting. Dust with powdered sugar before serving.

White Bean Beer Chili

Add 1 lb. ground turkey to a large pot over medium heat; break into small pieces while cooking. Add 1 chopped white onion and 3 diced jalapeños; cook until softened. Add 1 (12 oz.) bottle **light lager** and 2 C. chicken broth, scraping to deglaze the pan. Add 4 (15 oz.) cans great Northern beans *(drained and rinsed)*, ¼ tsp. garlic powder, ¼ tsp. paprika, ½ tsp. chipotle powder, ¼ tsp. cumin, ¼ tsp. chili powder, and ¼ tsp. oregano. Simmer for 10 minutes. Remove from heat, stir in 1 C. sour cream and season to taste with salt and black pepper. Ladle into bowls and top with shredded cheddar cheese and cilantro. *serves 8*

Serves 4

Beer-Doused Burgers

1 T. olive oil

1 T. butter

1 large Vidalia onion, thinly sliced

½ tsp. minced garlic

1 tsp. dried thyme

2 lbs. ground beef

½ tsp. salt

½ tsp. black pepper

1 (12 oz.) bottle **BROWN ALE**

1 tsp. balsamic vinegar

1 T. steak sauce

½ tsp. Dijon mustard

4 slices provolone cheese

Melt the olive oil and butter in a large skillet over medium heat. Add the onions, garlic, and thyme to the skillet and cook, stirring occasionally, until the onions begin to soften.

While the onions are cooking, season the ground beef with salt and pepper and form it into four patties. Push the softened onions to the outer edge of the skillet and add the burgers to the skillet. Cook the burgers for 2 to 3 minutes and then flip over. Add the brown ale, vinegar, steak sauce, and mustard to the pan and gently stir to combine.

Continue cooking the burgers to your desired doneness. Remove burgers from the skillet and continue to reduce the remaining liquid until it reaches a gravy-like consistency.

Serve the burgers on buns and top each with caramelized onions, provolone cheese, and the brown ale reduction.

Beer-Simmered Corn

Bring 4 (12 oz.) bottles of **light lager** to a boil in a large pot. Add 3 T. butter, ½ tsp. salt, and ½ tsp. seafood seasoning. Add 6 ears of corn and reduce heat to low. Cover and cook, turning occasionally, until corn is tender, about 15 minutes. Serve with butter, salt, black pepper, and lime wedges for drizzling.
serves 6

Makes 12

Raspberry Ale Shortcake

Preheat the oven to 400°. Mix 4 C. biscuit baking mix,
½ C. sugar, 1 T. lemon juice, and 1 (12 oz.) bottle **AMBER
ALE**. Pour into 12 greased muffin tins. Bake for 15 to
20 minutes, or until a toothpick comes out clean.

For the sauce, combine 2 C. fresh raspberries, 1 C. sugar, and
1 C. **AMBER ALE** in a saucepan over medium-high heat.
Allow to simmer, stirring occasionally, until reduced and
thickened, about 20 minutes. Spoon the sauce over the
shortcakes, top with whipped cream, and enjoy!

Makes 18

Cheesy Beer Puffs

Preheat the oven to 425°. Line a rimmed baking sheet with parchment paper. In a food processor, pulse 1¼ C. shredded cheddar, ¼ C. cream cheese, ¼ C. **AMBER ALE**, 1 tsp. bourbon, and 1 tsp. each paprika and garlic powder, scraping the bowl occasionally. Season to taste with salt and black pepper.

Unfold the thawed sheets from 1 (17 oz.) pkg. puff pastry. Cut each sheet into nine 3" squares. Spoon some cheese mixture onto half of each pastry square, leaving a ½" rim. Beat 1 egg with 1 T. water and brush a little on the rim of a pastry square. Fold the square in half to form a triangle; seal the edges with the tines of a fork. Repeat with the remaining pastry squares. Transfer to the baking sheet and brush with the egg mixture. Bake for 20 minutes or until golden brown.

Serves a crowd

Ine-brie-ated Onion Dip

1 large Vidalia onion
1 T. unsalted butter
1 T. olive oil
½ C. **PORTER**, divided
1 (8 oz.) pkg. brie
1 tsp. dried thyme

1 tsp. chopped fresh chives
1 T. honey
1 (8 oz.) pkg. cream cheese, softened
1 T. cornstarch
Baguette, sliced

Thinly slice the onion and put into a pot over medium heat with the butter and olive oil. Cook until the onions start to soften, and then add ¼ cup porter.

Cook over medium heat, stirring occasionally, until the onions turn dark brown and the beer has evaporated. Add the additional beer and cook until the pot only has about 2 tablespoons of liquid left.

Trim the rind off the brie and cut it into small cubes. Stir together the thyme, chives, honey, brie, cream cheese, and cornstarch.

Remove and discard the rind from the brie. Cube the cheese and mix it with the thyme, chives, honey, cream cheese, and cornstarch.

Bake at 375° for 15 minutes or until the cheese is bubbly; stir to combine. Serve warm with baguette slices.

Beery Mary

Rub the rim of a pint glass with a lime wedge; dip into coarse sea salt. In the glass, combine 6 oz. tomato juice, juice of ¼ lime, a dash each of hot sauce and Worcestershire sauce, ½ tsp. celery salt, and 6 oz. *light lager*. Stir and add ice to fill. Garnish with a lime wedge and olives. Serves 1

Prosciutto & Por

Prosciutto & Porter Fettucine

3 T. olive oil

3 oz. prosciutto

1 shallot, thinly sliced

1 lb. baby bella
   mushrooms, thinly sliced

1 tsp. minced garlic

1 tsp. dried thyme

⅓ C. **PORTER**

½ C. chicken broth

⅓ C. heavy cream

½ tsp. salt

½ tsp. black pepper

12 oz. fettucine pasta

¼ C. freshly grated
   Parmesan

Heat the olive oil in a large skillet over medium-high heat. Add the slices of prosciutto, cooking until crispy. Remove prosciutto from skillet; drain and set aside to cool.

Reduce heat to medium; add the shallot and cook until softened. Add the mushrooms, garlic, and thyme and cook until the mushrooms have browned, about 10 minutes.

Pour in the porter, scraping to deglaze the bottom of the pan. Stir in the chicken broth, lower the heat, and simmer until the sauce thickens slightly. Stir in the cream, salt, and pepper.

Cook the pasta in boiling, salted water until nearly al dente.

Drain the pasta and add it to the sauce. Toss to coat.

Transfer the pasta to a serving bowl. Top with crumbled posciutto and grated Parmesan.

Serves 4

Cheesy Beer Mashed Taters

Peel and cut 4 medium Yukon gold potatoes into quarters and place them in a large saucepan; add enough water to cover. Bring to a boil and reduce heat to medium-low; cover loosely and boil gently for 15 to 20 minutes or until the potatoes are tender. Drain and mash potatoes until no lumps remain. Add ¼ C. **AMERICAN LAGER** in small amounts, beating after each addition. Add ½ tsp. garlic salt, 2 T. butter, ¼ C. sour cream, ½ C. shredded cheddar, and 2 T. chopped chives. Mash until potatoes are light and fluffy. Season to taste with salt and black pepper.

Makes 20

Battered Buffalo Shrooms

Rinse and pat dry 1 lb. of white button mushrooms. Line a rimmed baking sheet with foil and set a cooling rack over it. Heat 2" of canola oil to 350° in a heavy saucepan. In a large bowl, mix 2 C. all-purpose flour, ¾ C. milk, 1 egg, ½ tsp. salt, and 1 (12 oz.) bottle **AMERICAN LAGER** until smooth. Dip the mushrooms into the batter and carefully set them into the hot oil. Fry until brown on all sides and transfer to the cooling rack. Repeat with the remaining mushrooms.

For the dipping sauce, melt ½ C. butter in a small saucepan over medium heat. Stir in ½ C. buffalo sauce, 2 T. American lager, and 1 tsp. brown sugar. Simmer for 1 to 2 minutes.

Serves 8-10

Brews-Key Lime Pie

2 sleeves graham crackers

½ C. unsalted butter, melted

2 tsp. plus 1 C. sugar, divided

3 (8 oz.) pkgs. cream cheese, softened

1 C. **LIME FLAVORED LAGER**

2 T. lime juice

3 eggs

Whipped cream

Lime zest

Preheat oven to 350°. Mix the graham crackers, butter, and 2 teaspoons sugar in a food processor until crumbled and fully combined. Clean out the food processor and add the cream cheese, lime flavored lager, lime juice, eggs, and the remaining 1 cup sugar. Blend the filling ingredients until fully mixed and smooth.

Grease a 9" springform pan and line the bottom with parchment paper. Pour the graham cracker mixture into the pan and press into the bottom and up the sides of the pan. Bake for 10 minutes. Remove from the oven and pour the filling into the pan. Bake for 1 hour. Turn off the oven and open the door for 5 minutes. Close the oven door and let the pie set for 30 minutes inside the oven.

Remove the pie from the oven and let it cool completely before removing the springform pan. Serve with whipped cream and lime zest.

The Lumberjack

*Mix 2 oz. apple flavored whiskey, the juice of ¼ lemon, and 1 oz. pure maple syrup until combined. Stir in 6 oz. **German-style hefeweizen** beer. Add ice to fill the glass and garnish with a twist of lemon peel. Now that's a drink suited for a lumberjack! Serves 1.*

37

Teriyaki Stout Beef

½ tsp. freshly grated ginger
1 tsp. Dijon mustard
¼ tsp. red pepper flakes
1 tsp. Sriracha sauce
1 tsp. minced garlic
¼ C. honey
1 T. brown sugar
½ tsp. black pepper

1 lb. flat iron steak
1 tsp. salt
¼ C. cornstarch
¼ C. **STOUT**
3 T. soy sauce
2 T. sesame oil
2 T. sesame seeds
2 T. chopped green onions

In a small bowl, stir together the ginger, mustard, red pepper flakes, Sriracha sauce, garlic, honey, brown sugar, and black pepper; set aside. Thinly slice the steak against the grain and sprinkle with salt.

Place the cornstarch in a small bowl and stir together the stout and soy sauce in a separate bowl.

Heat the sesame oil in a large skillet over medium heat.

A few at a time, dredge the beef strips in the cornstarch, dip into the beer mixture, and add to the skillet. Repeat with all of the beef.

Once the beef has started to brown, add the honey mixture as well as any of the remaining beer mixture to the skillet. Cook until sauce has thickened.

Top with sesame seeds and green onions and serve over rice.

 *Serves 8*

Brewer's Beans

½ lb. bacon, chopped

1 lb. lean ground beef

½ C. chopped white onion

1 (16 oz.) can black beans,
drained & rinsed

1 (16 oz.) can kidney beans,
drained & rinsed

1 (16 oz.) can butter beans,
drained & rinsed

1 (16 oz.) can baked beans

½ C. packed brown sugar

1 C. **AMERICAN LAGER**

⅓ C. ketchup

2 tsp. apple cider vinegar

1 tsp. Dijon mustard

1 tsp. chipotle powder

¼ tsp. garlic powder

¼ tsp. black pepper

In a large skillet, cook the bacon over medium heat until crisp. Transfer to paper towels to drain and cool; discard the drippings. In the same skillet, cook the beef and onion over medium heat until the meat is no longer pink; drain the drippings.

Stir together the beef mixture, bacon, beans, brown sugar, American lager, ketchup, vinegar, mustard, chipotle powder, garlic powder, and black pepper. Transfer to a 9 x 13" baking dish and bake, uncovered, at 325° for 45 to 60 minutes or until the beans are as thick as desired.

Liquid Courage Cornbread

Preheat the oven to 350º.

Combine 1 C. all-purpose flour, 1 C. cornmeal, 4 tsp. baking powder, and ½ tsp. salt in a large bowl. In a separate bowl, whisk together 1 egg, ½ C. milk, ½ C. **light lager**, and 2 T. honey; add to the cornmeal mixture and stir until just blended. Pour into a greased 8 x 8" pan. Bake for 20 minutes or until the top is lightly browned and a toothpick inserted in the center comes out clean. *serves 8*

Serves 4

Chicken Beersala

- ¾ C. flour
- 1 tsp. salt
- 1 tsp. black pepper
- 4 boneless, skinless chicken breasts
- 2 T. butter
- 1 T. olive oil
- 1½ C. thinly sliced white button mushrooms

- ⅓ C. thinly sliced red onion
- 1 tsp. minced garlic
- 1 tsp. dried thyme
- 1 (12 oz.) bottle **PORTER**
- 1½ C. chicken stock
- ½ C. shredded mozzarella cheese

In a shallow dish, mix the flour, salt, and pepper until combined. Coat both sides of each chicken breast in the flour mixture and shake off any excess.

Melt the butter and olive oil in a large skillet over medium-high heat. Brown both sides of the chicken breasts in the hot oil for 2 to 3 minutes; set aside while you make the sauce.

Add the mushrooms and onion to the same skillet; sauté for 2 to 3 minutes. Add the garlic and thyme and sauté for 1 minute more.

Pour the porter over the mushrooms and gently scrape the brown bits from the pan. Reduce the sauce about 3 minutes and add the chicken stock.

Reduce for another 6 to 7 minutes and return the chicken to the pan. Lower the heat to medium and simmer until the chicken is cooked through, about 12 minutes. Sprinkle with mozzarella and let melt before removing the chicken from the skillet.

Ale-Glazed Carrots & Walnuts

Wash and peel 1 lb. of fresh carrots; cut into ½" slices. Melt 3 T. butter in a large saucepan over medium heat. Add the carrots and 1 C. **amber ale** and bring to a boil. Reduce the heat so the beer bubbles gently; add 1 T. maple syrup. Simmer for 15 minutes, stirring occasionally, until the carrots are almost cooked through. Stir in ½ C. walnut halves and cook for 5 more minutes, or until the glaze is reduced to a couple of tablespoons. *serves 4*

IPA Sriracha Wings

2 lbs. chicken drumettes
   and wingettes

3½ C. **IPA**, divided

1 T. salt

¾ C. ketchup

½ C. Sriracha sauce

1 T. apple cider vinegar

2 T. soy sauce

1 tsp. freshly ground ginger

1 tsp. Worcestershire sauce

1 T. cornstarch

Combine the chicken drumettes and wingettes, 3 cups IPA, and salt in a plastic container and refrigerate for at least 3 hours.

Preheat the oven to 350°. Drain the wings and spread out on a greased rimmed baking sheet. Bake until cooked through, about 35 minutes.

If you like your wings extra crispy, broil them for 3 to 4 minutes, until the skin is golden brown and delicious.

In a small saucepan, combine the remaining ½ cup IPA with ketchup, Sriracha sauce, vinegar, soy sauce, ginger, Worcestershire, and cornstarch. Bring to a simmer. When the wings are done, toss them with the sauce while hot.

Serve with ranch dressing for dipping.

Grapefruit Shandy

In a large glass, combine 6 oz. ruby red grapefruit juice and 6 oz. Belgian-style white ale and add ice to fill. Garnish with a grapefruit wedge and fresh mint. If you're feeling adventurous, try swapping the grapefruit juice with lemonade or limeade for a refreshing twist. Serves 1

Serves 8

Jalapeño Cheddar Beer Bread

3 C. all-purpose flour

¼ C. sugar

¼ tsp. garlic salt

1 T. baking powder

2 jalapeños

1 C. shredded cheddar cheese, divided

1 (12 oz.) bottle **LIGHT LAGER**

¼ C. Chipotle Beer Butter *(recipe on page 47)*

Preheat oven to 350° and grease a 5 x 9" loaf pan. Sift the flour into a large bowl; add the sugar, garlic salt, and baking powder and stir until combined. Remove the seeds and membranes from the jalapeños and finely dice. Add the diced jalapeños and ¾ cup cheddar cheese to the mixture. Pour the light lager over the mixture and stir until well mixed.

Transfer the dough into the greased loaf pan and pour melted butter over the top. Bake for 30 minutes, then sprinkle with the remaining ¼ cup cheddar cheese and bake for 25 minutes more. Serve with Chipotle Beer Butter.

No yeast needed. The carbonation in the beer makes the bread light and fluffy. Which means this is the easiest homemade bread you'll ever make!

Chipotle Beer Butter

With an electric mixer, whip ½ C. softened butter until smooth and fluffy. Add 2 minced chipotle peppers in adobo, 1 T. adobo sauce from the can, 2 T. **light lager**, the juice of 1 lime, and 1 T. chopped cilantro to the mixture. Whip until incorporated. *makes about ¾ cup*

Serves 4-5

Brew-Schetta Pulled Pork

Place a 1½ to 2 lb. pork tenderloin into a slow cooker.

Whisk together 1 (12 oz.) bottle **PORTER**, ⅓ C. balsamic vinegar, 1 tsp. dried basil, 1 tsp. salt, 1 tsp. black pepper, ½ tsp. garlic powder, ½ tsp. dried oregano, ½ tsp. dried thyme, and ¼ C. brown sugar and pour the mixture over the tenderloin.

Cook on low for 6 to 7 hours or until the meat is cooked through and easily pulls apart. Shred the meat and serve on ciabatta rolls with sliced red onion, tomato, fresh mozzarella, and fresh basil.

Serves 4

Tirami-Brew

With and electric mixer, whip 1 (8 oz.) pkg. softened cream cheese and gently fold in 2 C. whipped topping *(thawed)*. In a shallow pie dish or bowl, stir together ½ C. **STOUT** and ½ C. brewed coffee. Quickly dip a few vanilla wafers into the coffee mixture and place in the bottom of an individual serving dish or cup. Carefully spread 2 heaping spoonfuls of the cream cheese mixture on top of the soaked wafers; sprinkle with ½ to 1 tsp. cocoa powder. Repeat two more times to make 3 layers, but on the final layer add just a light dusting of cocoa powder on top. Repeat the process for each individual dish.

Bacon & Ale Pecan Salad

6 bacon strips, chopped

1 C. packed brown sugar

1 T. salt

1 tsp. black pepper

⅓ C. **BELGIAN-STYLE WHITE ALE**

1½ C. pecan halves

8 C. assorted greens

½ gala apple, cored & thinly sliced

¼ C. blue cheese crumbles

¼ C. sliced red onion

¼ C. Balsamic Ale Vinaigrette *(recipe on page 51)*

Preheat the oven to 350° and grease a rimmed baking sheet with cooking spray. Sauté the bacon until crisp; drain and set aside to cool. In a small saucepan over medium heat, combine the brown sugar, salt, pepper, and Belgian-style white ale; let boil for 10 minutes, stirring often. Add the pecans and bacon and stir until coated; spread on the greased baking sheet. Bake for 16 to 18 minutes, turning occasionally. Remove from the oven and allow to cool before breaking apart.

For the salad, add the assorted greens to a large bowl and top with apple, blue cheese, red onion, and ½ cup of the toasted bacon and pecan mixture. Add the vinaigrette and toss to coat.

Save any leftover bacon and pecan mixture... it makes a great snack!

Balsamic Ale Vinaigrette

In a food processor or blender, process 1 C. **Belgian-style white ale**, 1 minced garlic clove, 1 T. honey, 1 tsp. Dijon mustard, 1 tsp. black pepper, ⅓ C. olive oil, and ½ C. balsamic vinegar until combined. *makes 2 cups*

Serves 4

Drunken Shrimp Stir-Fry

1 T. olive oil

1 T. butter

½ C. chopped yellow onion

½ to ⅔ C. **AMBER ALE**

2 T. tomato paste

2 tsp. Sriracha sauce

2 tsp. honey

1 tsp. brown sugar

1 tsp. soy sauce

1 tsp. sesame seeds

1 (12 oz.) pkg. raw shrimp, thawed, peeled, deveined & patted dry

1½ C. sugar snap peas

Fresh cilantro

Cooked rice

In a large skillet, heat the oil and butter until melted. Add the onion and cook until soft. Add the amber ale, tomato paste, Sriracha sauce, honey, brown sugar, soy sauce, and sesame seeds and bring to a boil.

Once boiling, add the shrimp and peas. Cook for 3 minutes; flip and cook another 3 minutes or until the shrimp is pink, cooked through, and curled up. Garnish with fresh cilantro and serve over rice.

You can tell when a shrimp is done not only by its pink color, but also by its shape. If it looks like a "U" it's undercooked; an "O" means it's overcooked; and a "C" means it's correct.

Raspberry Bliss

*In a large cocktail glass, muddle ¼ C. fresh raspberries and 2 tsp. sugar. Add ½ oz. vodka and stir to combine; top with 6 oz. **IPA** and add ice to fill. Garnish with a fresh raspberry. Now that's a refreshing cocktail! Serves 1*

Serves 4-5

Rosemary Beer Chicken

1 T. dried rosemary
1 tsp. dried sage
3 T. olive oil
1 T. honey mustard
1 T. honey
½ tsp. salt

½ tsp. black pepper
1 tsp. minced garlic
1 (12 oz.) bottle
  BROWN ALE
2 lbs. chicken drumsticks

Whisk together the rosemary, sage, olive oil, mustard, honey, salt, pepper, garlic, and brown ale in a large bowl or baking dish. Add the chicken and turn to coat; cover and refrigerate for at least 1 hour.

Preheat the oven to 375°.

Spread the chicken on a foil-lined rimmed baking sheet. Bake at 375° for 45 minutes until the chicken is cooked through and the skin is crispy. Yum!

Sweet Potato Ale Fries

Preheat oven to 450°. Scrub 3 lbs. sweet potatoes and cut into ½" slices; cut the slices into french fry shapes. In a large bowl, soak the cut fries in 12 oz. **brown ale** for 20 minutes, tossing 1 or 2 times. Drain the beer and toss the fries with 2 T. olive oil, 1 tsp. minced garlic, 1 tsp. dried rosemary, 1 tsp. salt, and ½ tsp. black pepper until well coated. Spread a single layer of fries on a rimmed baking sheet. Bake for 45 minutes to 1 hour, depending on how crispy you like them, turning 2 or 3 times. *serves 6*

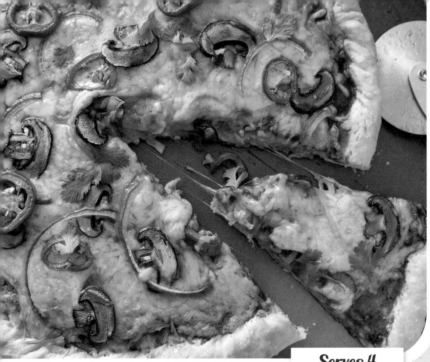

Serves 4

BeerBQ Pizza

3 C. all-purpose flour, plus more for dusting

1 T. baking powder

½ tsp. salt

1 (12 oz.) can **LIGHT LAGER**

1 T. olive oil

½ C. Kickin' Stout BBQ *(recipe on page 57)*

2 C. shredded Gouda cheese

Sliced red onion

Flamin' Beer Jalapeños *(recipe on page 9)*

Sliced baby bella mushrooms

Fresh cilantro

Preheat oven to 450°.

Combine the flour, baking powder, and salt in a large bowl and mix thoroughly.

Pour in the light lager and mix until combined *(the dough will be sticky)*. Sprinkle the outside of the dough with flour and form a ball. Grease a pizza pan with cooking spray and use a rolling pin to roll the dough into a circle. Roll and crimp the edges of the dough to create a crust; brush the dough with olive oil and poke a few holes with a fork.

Bake for 10 minutes and remove from the oven. Top with the Kickin' Stout BBQ, Gouda cheese, red onion, jalapeños, and mushrooms to taste. Bake for an additional 10 minutes or until golden brown on top. Garnish with cilantro.

Kickin' Stout BBQ

Heat 1 T. olive oil in a saucepan over medium heat and stir in 1 tsp. minced garlic. Add ¼ C. soy sauce, 2 T. tomato paste, 2 T. ketchup, 2 T. Worcestershire sauce, 2 T. apple cider vinegar, 1 tsp. chipotle powder, ½ tsp. onion powder, 1 C. stout, and ½ C. packed brown sugar; cook until thickened, stirring occasionally. *makes 1½ cups*

Stout-Glazed Salmon & Shrooms

2 lbs. whole white button
  mushrooms

2 shallots, sliced

1 tsp. dried thyme

1 C. **STOUT**, divided

2 T. olive oil

½ tsp. coarse sea salt,
  divided

½ tsp. black pepper,
  divided

2 T. packed brown sugar

1 tsp. Dijon mustard

4 (6 oz.) salmon fillets

Preheat the oven to 400°.

In a large bowl, combine the mushrooms, shallots, thyme, and
¼ cup stout; drizzle with oil, season with ¼ teaspoon
each salt and pepper, and toss to combine. Arrange the
mushroom mixture in a single layer on a large rimmed
baking sheet. Roast the mushrooms, stirring 2 or 3 times,
for 20 minutes. Remove from the oven and set aside.

Meanwhile, in a small saucepan, stir together the brown
sugar, mustard, and remaining ¾ cup stout and bring the
mixture to a boil. Reduce the heat and simmer for 5 to
8 minutes or until the liquid is reduced to about ½ cup.
Remove from the heat and set the glaze aside. Reserve
half of the glaze for serving.

Pat the fish dry and season with the remaining ¼ teaspoon
each salt and pepper. Place skin-side down in a large baking
dish. Toss the roasted mushrooms with 2 tablespoons of the
glaze and arrange them around fish; drizzle with any juice
in the pan. Brush the fish with an additional 2 tablespoons
of the glaze. Roast until the fish is just cooked through
and flakes easily, about 10 to 13 minutes. Serve with the
reserved glaze on the side.

Drunken Salsa

Preheat a skillet to medium-high; place 5 Roma tomatoes and 2 jalapeño peppers in the skillet and roast for 3 minutes. Then add 1 garlic clove and ½ C. chopped white onion to the skillet; continue roasting the vegetables, turning occasionally, until they become slightly charred and soft. Let the vegetables cool slightly before removing the stems from the jalapeños; if you prefer a milder salsa, remove the seeds and membranes as well. Transfer the charred vegetables to a food processor; add ½ C. **LIGHT LAGER**, 1 tsp. salt, ¼ tsp. black pepper, and the juice of 2 limes. Pulse until the mixture is coarsely chopped. Stir in ½ C. chopped cilantro and serve with tortilla chips.

Serves 5

No-Churn Toffee & Stout Ice Cream

Add 1½ C. heavy cream, ⅓ C. sugar, and ½ C. powdered sugar to a mixing bowl. Beat together on high until soft peaks form.

Add 3 T. cocoa powder, ½ tsp. salt, and ½ C. toffee bits and mix until combined.

While the mixer is running, slowly pour ¼ C. **STOUT** into the bowl and mix until well combined. Transfer to a freezer-safe container and freeze until set, about 7 hours.

Serves 5

Cerveza Tortilla Soup

1 (14.5 oz.) can fire-roasted diced tomatoes

1 (12 oz.) bottle **AMERICAN LAGER**

4 C. chicken broth

½ tsp. chipotle powder

½ tsp. ground cumin

½ tsp. onion powder

1 tsp. chili powder

1 tsp. garlic powder

½ tsp. red pepper flakes

½ tsp. salt

1 lb. boneless, skinless chicken breasts

Cilantro

Avocado

Cotija cheese

Tortilla chips

Put the tomatoes and American lager into a food processor and pulse until well combined.

Transfer the mixture to a large pot over medium-high heat along with the broth, chipotle powder, ground cumin, onion powder, chili powder, garlic powder, red pepper flakes, and salt. Bring to a simmer and add the chicken to the pot to cook. Once the chicken is cooked through, about 20 minutes, shred the chicken and add it back to the soup.

Top each bowl of soup with cilantro, diced avocado, crumbled cotija cheese, and tortilla chips.

Throwin' a fiesta? Set out a variety of toppings and let guests top their own bowls!

Citrus Brewshie Sangria

*Wash and thinly slice 1 grapefruit, 1 navel orange, 1 lime, and 1 lemon. Combine the sliced fruit, 16 oz. pineapple juice, and 8 oz. vodka in a large pitcher. Refrigerate for at least 2 hours. When you're ready to serve, add 3 (12 oz.) bottles **Belgian-style white ale** to the fruit mixture. Serve over ice. **serves 8***

Index